Gravitas

Reimagining The Sunday Lecture Model
Restoring Jesus' Conversational Model!

a summary for church leaders from the book
Life, Love & Leading

Gravitas

To receive additional free copies please contact:
Ricky Kroeger
One Kingdom Worldwide
OneKingdomWorldwide.org

Revised March 2026

All scripture is English Standard Version (ESV) unless otherwise indicated.

Chapter One

Who Will Reverse The Trend?

A Barna Group study in 2007 found that there is very little difference between the lifestyles & behaviors of people who call themselves Christian and those who do not. The evidence from work done by Pew Research and Gallup regarding people in the USA makes it clear that things are only getting worse:

- In 2000, 90% believed in God. In 2022 that number was 81%.
- In 2005, 79% were convinced that God exists. In 2017 that number was 64%.
- In 1971, 90% identified as Christian. In 2008: 77%. In 2019: 65%
- Between 2009-2019, the percentage of Christians who say they attend church regularly dropped 7%.
- Half of all Christians say they attend church once or twice each month.
- Half of all Christians say they only attend church a few times per year or less.
- In 1999, 73% were members of a church. In 2019 that number was 47%.
- In 2009, 17% identified as atheist, agnostic or "nothing in particular". In 2019: 26%.

Given that half of all Christians say they only attend church a few times per year or less, another study tried to determine the percentage of believers who take the Great Commission of making disciples seriously. Their results? 7%.

What do we have wrong? The evidence is clear. Who will reverse the trend? *Something must be wrong with our approach*. Check the math, our task is not all that daunting. Using the 7% number from above, if *each* year *each* Christ follower will invest themselves in the life of *one person they know* who is not yet a true follower - within 4 years the entire USA will have had the opportunity to secure their eternity.

Each One Reach One Each Year:

- In Year 1: the 7% becomes 14%
- In Year 2: the 14% becomes 28%
- In Year 3: the 28% becomes 56%
- During Year 4: the 56% becomes 100%

Introduction

In Jesus' day, the clear responsibility of the rabbi was to teach them "how to fulfill the Torah". That is to say, "how to live a life pleasing to God". Jesus came to live it out and *engrain it conversationally* as an example. We have lost our way in this. We have left behind the *conversational* model Jesus used with the twelve for the *lecture* model he used with the masses from a mountainside or a boat just offshore. As Jesus piqued the curiosity of the crowd in these, *individuals* were drawn closer for the *deeper* conversations.

As the twelve became proficient through the *life-on-life* time Jesus afforded *them*, they were then able to do the same in support of the 70 and the 500. "Hey, John, Jesus is surrounded by people asking him questions and I can't get close to him. You are one of his guys, what does he have to say about this…?", thereby initiating a *life-on-life* opportunity for *them*!

Just like with you, there was not enough time in the day for Jesus to disciple every person around him! More importantly, how many cannot get to *you* and eventually give up on asking their questions because there is no one else to ask? Without 12 of your own, and a high level of visibility and recognition of who your 12 are, how many walk away - and we lose our chance to grow *them*? Not only them, but the 70 and the 500!

Please read this summary of *Life, Love and Leading*. These were written to support your discipleship and development efforts and are available free in the downloadable pdf at OneKingdomWorldwide.org.

Life has been used effectively for many years with individuals and in small group bible studies with people from all walks of life: the poor, the rich, the homeless, present & former prison inmates, struggling believers, wayward believers, in marital & pre-marital counseling, with friends, parents, pastors, mentors and teachers. *Life* helps us think about our conversations together with *hearts* after the Father, the *mind and attitudes* of Christ, *language and actions* that produce *fruit of the Spirit*, and *love* that proves we *care* and are *his*.

Love supports the individual prayer time needed in allowing God the Father, Son and Holy Spirit to *accomplish his sanctification* in our lives.

Leading helps us to build upon *Life* and *Love* collectively for family and community transformation. Scattered like salt across our communities and found, as Jesus was, *in service to one another*, each individual grain reflecting the light of God's love, *more and more people will be led into lifesaving relationship* – and our families and communities will be restored.

Preface

These are exciting days. Though for years and years we've been closing 16 churches every day here in the USA, we are now clearly at the dawn of a new awakening of God's people.

Over the last 20-30 years, the internet has made it possible for thousands of Christian scholars to peer review each other's work from anywhere in the world. Most importantly, this has led to their ability to collaborate, confirm, and identify essential original scriptural *context* that has been lost down through the ages. As you will see, these lost contexts from the time of Jesus, and of the 1st century church, are essential to our depth of understanding - and therefore to our success in making disciples.

One of the learnings assimilated for you here, is that church in the USA has been modeled after Europe's Hellenistic lecture model - not after the conversational model the Father prepared for the Son 100-150 years before the birth of Jesus. Another is that we simply *do not understand* what it means to be a *disciple* according to the Hebrew term for it in Jesus' day: *talmid.*

Using the conversational model the Father prepared in advance for the Son, Jesus' followers changed the world around them. But as they later expanded into Europe, the western Hellenistic cultural model of lecturing *swallowed them up*. A great many people were converted but it was not sustainable because it had lost the model the Father had prepared for the Son.

Now, the collapse of 16 churches every day here in the USA is following the cycle of the collapse of the church in Europe. If we don't learn from our history, we are condemned to repeat it.

I have been following the above mentioned peer reviewed scholarly material for over 20 years and recently noticed that it's being accepted by the seminaries of repute in our day. Since our scholars have found agreement, it's time for our seminaries, pastors, and families to be awakened to the fact that church decline has been occurring precisely because of the absence of such critically essential biblical *context*. This is foundational information upon which I believe all of the more than 250 denominations of the Christian church in the USA can agree.

I have been sharing these assimilations, these learnings, through what have become four books and a series of short videos understandable by any Christ follower with a general Bible background. It is so very important that we realize HOW we adopted the European Hellenistic Lecture model – and return instead to the conversational model the Father prepared for the Son.

Considering the world population, Pew Research states that 31% identify as Christian. Of them, perhaps we could say that 5% take the Great Commission of making disciples seriously. Doing the math again, assuming that every one of the 5% make just one true disciple each year, the entire world will have had the opportunity to secure their eternity within 5 years!

Each One Reach One Each Year:

- In Year 1: the 5% becomes 10%
- In Year 2: the 10% becomes 20%
- In Year 3: the 20% becomes 40%
- In Year 4: the 40% becomes 80%
- During Year 5: the 80% becomes 100%

Clearly, our problem is not in our numbers, but likely in that our approaches do not grow disciples who care – with hearts after the Father.

Where God's people are active in the *character and attitudes* of Jesus, *the will* of the Father and *as led* by the Spirit, Sigmoid Curves are the result. Now, after two thousand years, have we peaked? No, the data suggests that we are on the back side of a *Bell* Curve, backsliding *from* our peak. Is it not insanity that we continue to do what has brought us to this point? Let's go back to the era of Jesus to contemplate what we may be missing…

****

Given my desire to respect your time, church leader, and because of the substantial scriptural documentation available in the supportive book *Life, Love and Leading*, you will find the following chapters to be quick and direct. For your deeper consideration, please refer to *Life, Love and Leading,* available free in both the published version and downloadable pdf.

Please forgive my indulgence in brevity on your behalf as I do my best to get right to each point. Thank you in advance for your understanding.

Chapter Two

Before The Birth Of The Christ

Around 150-100 BC God was doing a new thing, but most Christians today do not perceive it. He was preparing the people of a small area of Israel (Bethsaida, Korazin and Capernaum) for the coming Messiah. This area, sometimes called The Triangle, developed a discipleship track that began with elementary school – Beth Sephir. There, they began teaching children to read and write using the Torah, and by the time they were twelve years old, *all* would have memorized most of it.

This was the beginning of a new thing, and it has been confirmed by a broad swath of historians. It had not previously existed within Israel, and was birthed at least a hundred years before Jesus' arrival in Galilee. In preparation. In the area of The Triangle.

After Beth Sephir, somewhere around the age of 12, most boys would go into the family trade and most girls into supporting family life. However, for those who really had a passion for the Word of God, they could instead go on to Beth Midrash. Beth Midrash included study and memorization of most of the rest of the Hebrew Bible (the Tanakh) and provided them opportunity to begin considering a rabbinic lifestyle.

If you completed Beth Midrash and wanted to continue on to become a rabbi, you would observe the various rabbis in the area and ask one of them if you could follow them. If the rabbi agreed, he would give you an opportunity to follow him everywhere he went to talk with him about the great and deep learnings, understandings and interpretations available in the Tanakh. If the rabbi rejected you at some point, you would likely go back and join the family trade.

If your rabbi gained confidence in you as you walked together, you would become a *talmid*, one of his talmidim (plural), and be on your way to becoming a rabbi following several years of training. The role of the rabbi was to "teach the people *how* to fulfill the Torah". That is to say, *how* to live a life pleasing to God. Spending every minute of every day with their rabbi, talmidim would watch and see and hear and learn *how* he helped people understand and fulfill the Torah. Both by his words and by his actions.

But what are talmidim? Talmidim are what we in the USA erroneously call disciples, students and apprentices:

> *A talmid is probably different than you think because we do not have any word for it in our English language. Unlike the words disciple or student or apprentice that suggest a learning and doing process, the word talmid is a Hebrew term that describes a becoming process. Talmidim desire to become just like their rabbi. It is more than the practical application of the knowledge gained. It is more than taking actions based upon our understanding of his teachings. A talmid of Rabbi Jesus will have a heart after the Father, be growing to reflect the very character of Jesus and be gaining the mind and attitudes of Christ.*

For those a rabbi accepted, the job of a follower was to *become* just like him. It was not just to know what the rabbi knew, but to *be* what the rabbi *was*.

On the Sabbath, all of the rabbis from the insulas of the town (often five or more rabbis with hundreds of people in attendance) would gather in the synagogue to *conversationally* consider the appointed text of that Sabbath day. There would be a reading or two from the Torah and/or Tanakh, and the reader could share a brief testimony regarding the scripture selections for the day. Then the people would listen to the rabbis discuss the text so as to enlighten them with their thoughts on the historical context, likely using related text, each including their interpretations - with respectful consideration of differing perspectives a common element.

With several rabbis present, no one rabbi could steer the people in an unhealthy direction over time. Because of Beth Sephir most people were Torah literate. Because of Beth Midrash, the many talmidim of the rabbis present were Tanakh literate.

Interestingly, it was culturally acceptable for *anyone* present to add to the discussion, request clarification in a related text, provide a testimony or even disagree with something that had been shared. In this way, the collective wisdom of *all* the people was available for consideration *by all the people*. In this way, faith was made more *personal*. In this way, the people learned *how* to fulfill the Torah, *how* to live a life pleasing to God.

In this way, children might hear a testimony from their uncle; or a grandfather their son; and in so doing create the opportunity to discuss it personally together later – expanding upon the learning and adding depth to what was shared.

In *conversational* style, God could send in his *Encouragers*, *Disruptors* or *Correctors* to contribute to the discussions and raise up issues and scripture for community deliberation. It was this setup that made it possible for Jesus (and later the apostle Paul) to speak *in any synagogue on any Sabbath*. This is also one of the reasons that young Jesus was able to speak and amaze so many of those present – in the years *before* he started his three-year ministry.

This, too, helps to explain why Andrew, Peter, James and John immediately dropped their nets and followed him when he called them (Matthew 4:18-22, Luke 5:1-11). All four were raised in the small fishing town of Bethsaida, probably played together, and must have witnessed young Jesus together in synagogue conversations on Sabbaths during the years prior!

Maybe more importantly regarding these four, what does it say about Jesus that *he went to them and called them?!!!* Remember, aspiring talmidim would customarily be required to *ask the rabbi if they may follow him*. What Jesus was saying to them was, "*I believe you can be like me! Come! Follow me, and I will make you fishers of men!*" Near the end of his ministry, he reminded them of this, "You did not choose me, but I chose you." (John 15:16)

He tells modern day believers that *he believes in us, too*, still saying, "Go, make *talmidim* of all nations…" It's not all about teaching *what* we are to *know*, but the *how* we are to *live* to *become like him*. As we adopt the *how*, we will more likely *desire to delve deeper into the scriptures* to learn more of the supportive *what*.

****

Though Jesus taught thousands from a boat or a mountainside, the teaching that changed the world started *both as a group and individually* with the twelve. I wonder how many of the twelve were eventually involved in ongoing life-on-life conversations with the 70, and how many of the 70 were involved in life-on-life conversations with the 500? I wonder how often it would happen that an inquiring mind could not ask their question of Jesus because he was so surrounded by others trying to do the same. I wonder how often they would then elect to ask their question of one of his talmidim, thereby initiating a life-on-life opportunity for *them*: "Hey, John, you are one of his guys, what does Jesus say, or maybe, what does Jesus think about this…?"

What I *do* know, is that Jesus was not involved in ongoing life-on-life conversations with all of the 70 or the 500. Just like for you, dear leader, there is simply not enough time in the day! More importantly, how many cannot get to *you* and eventually give up on asking their questions because there is no one else to ask?

Without a high level of visibility and recognition of who your 12 are, how many walk away – and we lose our chance to grow them? If your 12 are frequently speaking in the weekly conversational opportunities, the inquirer will far more easily start with one of *them* if they cannot get to *you*, as in the above example.

Moreover, if you have described to your congregation that your 12 are highly capable of pastoring people through the troubles of life, and that you will be Connecting those that approach you with one of *them* - you will only have the 12 with whom to focus. Then, like Moses' father-in-law advised (Exodus 18:13-27), any additional load will come almost entirely from those your 12 have first screened, vetted or have previously attempted to support.

Clearly, Jesus' way was to make talmidim who would make talmidim. Do you have twelve or so that get *that* kind of time with *you*? Do you add to their numbers each year as *they* participate with you to develop *more* talmidim? The 70, and then the 500? The church leaders I know who *do* have been sending highly impactful service minded talmidim into their communities as yeast, salt and light for decades – and as they serve those in need, they use those opportunities to make more talmidim!

His <u>three-year</u> focus on training the 12 set into motion their activity with the 70, them with the 500 and the making of talmidim in every nation on earth.

Our people have been going to church for 5, 10, 20, 30, 40 years and more. If we have been making talmidim, most would *be* mature talmidim by now and be out making talmidim who are making talmidim who are making talmidim… and we would not be closing a net of eight churches each day here in the USA. They should *be* mature talmidim by now…

Hebrews 5:11-6:3

11 About this we have much to say, and it is hard to explain, since you have become dull of hearing. 12 For though by this time you ought to be teachers, you need someone to teach you again the basic principles of the oracles of God. You need milk, not solid food, 13 for everyone who lives on milk is unskilled in the word of righteousness, since he is a child. 14 But solid food is for the mature, for those who have their powers of discernment trained by constant practice to distinguish good from evil. 6:1-3 Therefore let us leave the elementary doctrine of Christ and go on to maturity, not laying again a foundation of repentance from dead works and of faith toward God, 2 and of instruction about washings, the laying on of hands, the resurrection of the dead, and eternal judgment. 3 And this we will do if God permits.

****

When Jesus said go and make talmidim of all nations, he did not say go and teach people Beth Sephir and Beth Midrash (the Tanakh) so that they could practically apply the information to their lives, he said to go help people *become* like him! Between the *what to know* and the *how to live*, he spent more time on the *how – how to live a life pleasing to God.*

Following Jesus' resurrection, the bible indicates that there were small rabbinic/talmidic style Sabbath gatherings that met in homes and *went out to serve locally* through the week. This service developed relational connections that could lead to the sharing of the love of God, the fellowship of the believers and invitations to join them.

Do your small groups go out in service-minded ways that create relational opportunities to *teach the people how to live a life pleasing to God?* That was the role of the rabbi in Jesus' day, that is what Rabbi Jesus and his talmidim did – and that is what we are to be doing. In this way, the ekklesia (or ecclesia) are effective in serving, sharing and inviting for the making of more and more talmidim.

These days our English bible translations use the word "church" where the Greek shows ekklesia. Ancient language historians indicate that this word actually means "called out". This is significant. Jesus set them apart and called them out of the darkness to reflect the light of God to the people of the world.

Today, if you ask someone what the followers of Jesus do, the answer would likely be "Go to church.". Yet if you could ask 1st century followers of Jesus what they did, the answer would likely be "Go out into the community in acts of service, for the development of relationships and opportunities to share.".

Also preaching in community settings as Jesus and Paul did, they piqued the curiosity of people such that the development of additional rabbinic/talmidic type conversational "small groups" could be initiated. Their goal? To teach them *how to live a life pleasing to God*, that they might become talmidim who make talmidim who make talmidim.

Two thousand years later, we have lost the context of this and many other portions of scripture. Because we are not from that era, we have also lost the images those words would immediately evoke culturally in their listeners. But how did it happen?

The Beginning of our Tradition of Preaching

Imagine with me: In the centuries after Jesus' resurrection, as the ekklesia "went out" to the cities of Europe, they found themselves *surrounded* by the western culture. In it, the Hellenistic Lecture Model was the most *culturally* accepted form of teaching. Given their desire to reach the masses, and their personal unfamiliarity with the Hebrew rabbinic/talmidic culture of Jesus' day, it is no wonder that they would adopt the build a bigger "church" concept. As preaching alone became their norm, it took away the possibility that *anyone else* might speak. In so doing, it lost one of the great potential benefits of the *conversational* style - God could no longer send in his *Encouragers*, *Disruptors* or *Correctors* to contribute to the discussions and raise up issues and scripture for community deliberation.

Without a focus upon developing *12 or so talmidim first*, as Jesus did, there was not a sufficient number of talmidim around to grow the 70 and the 500. And since it was not possible for *anyone else* to speak, it also became possible for the *singular* person/pastor/teacher to steer the people in an unhealthy direction over time.

Our Build-A-Bigger-Church Culture seemed necessary so as to gather the masses in one place each week to enable times of teaching and communion by the few. Therefore, absent the conversational rabbinic/talmidic life-on-life learning style, it traditionalized their inability to make true talmidim. Since the depth of understanding required individually could not be imparted rabbinically/talmidically, the traditionalized Lecture model further engrained GOING to church to hear – and passed it down these very many centuries.

As well intentioned "followers" passed along their limited understandings, errors were passed down generationally. Hardly the conversational life-on-life talmidic multiplication that Jesus exhibited, Europe is now littered with huge empty cathedrals… and now *we in the USA* are closing 16 churches every day.

Let's return "church" to the Conversational Synagogue Learning Way
If *we* will endeavor to *become* like Jesus, the making of talmidim will require *individual* conversational time in ongoing *life-on-life* discussion. Not forsaking the fellowship, a talmid will also be associated with some sort of *group* of talmidim - continually discussing *how to become more and more like Jesus*. Not only that, but *how to help others understand what it means* to live a life pleasing to God in *their* becoming. This bears repeating:

When Jesus said go and make talmidim of all nations, he did not say go and teach people Beth Sephir and Beth Midrash (the Tanakh), he said to go help them <u>become like him</u>! As with Jesus, the making of talmidim requires individual conversational time in life-on-life discussion.

His yolk is easy and his burden is light. It is much easier to focus on twelve or so than it is to take responsibility for a whole "church" *en masse*. God will bring the increase if we will return to the *conversational Synagogue way*.

Matthew 11:28-30
28 Come to me, all who labor and are heavy laden, and I will give you rest. 29 Take my yoke upon you, and learn from me, for I am gentle and lowly in heart, and you will find rest for your souls. 30 For my yoke is easy, and my burden is light."

The lone teacher setup is a heady situation that risks people becoming teacher followers rather than talmidim of Jesus. With several rabbis present, the collective wisdom of the elders would foster a deeper understanding. With several rabbis present, no one rabbi could steer the people in an unhealthy direction over time. With several rabbis and their talmidim present, individuals could more easily find one with whom they could have life-on-life conversations during the week.

In conversational style, God could send in his Encouragers, Disruptors or Correctors to contribute to the discussions and raise up issues and scripture for community deliberation. It was this setup that made it possible for Jesus (and later the apostle Paul) to speak in any synagogue on any Sabbath.

GO, make talmidim... people who are becoming like me, who GO like I went.

Dear pastor/teacher/elder/deacon: What have you produced? Are you making *mature talmidim*? By this time, after so very many years, *they* ought to be teachers now, too! (Hebrews 5:11-6:3) But perhaps they have simply become *your* followers, lacking the confidence to GO out, *with* him and *in* him, making more and more talmidim.

Instead, do they return to you each week to hear again and again the *what to know* and the promise of eternity? Where is their fruit beyond their offerings, their service in the fellowship and beyond their material contributions to people in need? How many are coming back in with joyful reports of *new* talmidim in the making? New talmidim who are learning *how to live a life pleasing to God* as they *become* more and more like Jesus!

A talmid of Rabbi Jesus will have a heart after the Father, be growing to reflect the very character of Jesus, be gaining the mind and attitudes of Christ – and have at least one person with whom they are discussing and describing how to live a life pleasing to God.

Chapter Three

Talmidic Or Hellenistic?

The Bible was written to the people of *that* day. It was not written *to* us, it was written *to them* and *for us*. Like the people of Jesus' day who knew the Torah and maybe even the whole Tanakh (the Old Testament), our people need help in grasping the depth and context of the people of the *biblical era* to better live a life pleasing to God today! For though they had been to Beth Sephir and Beth Midrash, the apostles still needed the same kind of help that *our* people do to *become* talmidim.

We admonish people to read their Bibles each day, and we teach them *what* the Bible says each week, but many are having difficulty with understanding the *how*. Like his talmidim, we need to have the *life of the Christ* opened up to us *in context* if we will *comprehend the how* of living the God-led life - with hearts after our Father, eyes that see and ears that hear. Otherwise, without *individual conversational time*, we are causing them to be always seeing, but never perceiving. (Matthew 13:14, Isaiah 6:9, Mark 4:12)

Like the two who encountered Jesus *conversationally* on the road to Emmaus (Luke 24:13-35), their hearts will burn as the scriptures are opened up to them. Jesus availed himself for 40 days after his resurrection to personalize the scriptures for his followers. He connected the scattered references to himself found in the Tanakh, identified the hundreds of prophecies about himself that he fulfilled, and clarified the story (his-story) so that they in turn could help others with *how* to live a life pleasing to God. And us for still others as well.

Like the story of Philip and the Eunuch (Acts 8:26-40), people need to have the scriptures opened up to them *conversationally* if they will *comprehend what they are reading.*

Like the story of Priscilla and Aquila pulling Apollos to the side *conversationally* for the deeper understanding (Acts 18:24-28), how will we support the passionate in passing along the *whole* Bible, context and all? Like Apollos, who eventually went to Achaia and powerfully and *conversationally* refuted the Jews in public, will our passionate people be fully prepared to *go*?

Much of what our present-day leaders do on Sundays *preaches* scripture so as to provide us *the what* head knowledge for *life application*. This is not the *talmidic* approach for *becoming like our Rabbi Jesus*, but rather the individualistic Hellenistic *lecture* approach which became common throughout Europe. The Greek word for this lecture or preaching approach, *homiletic*, found its origin in the 17th century as it became Europe's dominant approach for sharing the Gospel – but it was not and is not the model the Father prepared for the Son 100-150 years before Jesus' birth.

Now, just like Europe, littered with huge empty cathedrals, have we fallen victim to our lack of understanding of *the how* as we have attempted to *scale* via *homiletic lecture* as the family of God? According to ChurchLeadership.org, every year more than 4000 churches close their doors compared to just over 1000 new church starts. On average we are losing a net of eight churches each day!

The church in the USA was birthed by the talmidic families of God who escaped Europe in pursuit of freedom. Unfortunately, more and more have adopted the homiletic *preaching* path and process over these many centuries. Looking back, this just seemed to make more sense as our communities grew from small towns and villages of people who knew each other, into cities of the faceless and nameless!

At the city scale, our sermons have lost the conversational synagogue approach of Jesus' day. One of the reasons is because we are overwhelmed at the concept of individually teaching so many via life-on-life conversations: an impossible burden! Is it not now time to train the 12 he has given us, and them the 70 that he will give them - that we might have a chance with the 500? It was enough for Jesus…

Without ongoing life-on-life conversations individually, how can we expect them to comprehend *how* to live a life pleasing to God as a talmid?

Jesus was not involved in ongoing life-on-life conversations with all of the 70 or 500. Just like for you, there is simply not enough time in the day! Clearly, Jesus' way was to make talmidim who would make talmidim. Please, ask God to identify for you the first twelve or so that will begin to get that kind of group and individual time with you. Then add to their numbers each year as they then participate with you to develop more and more talmidim. The 70, and then the 500. The church leaders I know who have been doing this have been sending highly impactful service-minded talmidim into their communities as yeast, salt and light for decades – and are making more and more talmidim!

I believe that this homiletic *Tradition of Lecture* began to be passed down to the 3rd and the 4th generation in the USA more than a hundred years ago as our small towns and villages of people who knew each other grew into nameless and faceless cities, and that this is the biggest reason that the church has been in decline for so very many decades. While it is an indictment of the ways of our seminaries, Bible colleges, pastors, teachers and parenting down through the generations that our numbers have fallen off so drastically, the homiletic *lecture model* we now use almost exclusively was initially *a logical sounding seed Satan sowed in Deception* that we simply did not understand!

En masse, we tend to give people the facts and the logic and fight to persuade them for saving faith and helpful actions. Then, after baptism, continue our fact-filled logical Hellenistic *lecture* approach with weekly self-help Bible teaching and encouragements to serve. As we keep their brains engaged in thinking it all through - *without ongoing life-on-life opportunities in which to ask their questions, and lost in their heads* - many will walk away. Many *have* walked away, and so our families and nation are falling apart.

We would do well to reconsider our tradition of individuals teaching to gatherings by lecture. Rather, let's afford people conversational iron sharpening iron opportunities as Jesus and the apostles did.

****

What if we were to change our approach so as to better facilitate hearts after God with talmidim conversationally? What if we adopted the conversational synagogue method the Father prepared in advance for Jesus in the synagogues of The Triangle? What if all people had the opportunity to be involved in conversational learning in our Sunday services? What if our 12 were sufficiently trained to support the 70 and them the 500?

What if we were to instead *go* into our communities like Jesus *went,* to *pique the curiosity* of the people such that some came to our Sunday gatherings for *conversational* learning? What if the kind of teaching we do now on Sundays (like Jesus did from a boat or mountainside) happened instead in our community centers, our parks, our marketplaces, our homeless encampments and on our street corners?

What if denominationally disparate groups of pastor/teachers advertised a day each month where they would take turns using their current Sunday teaching gifts for several hours together in the local community center? What if *our* target audience was as *Jesus'* target audience was - and was supported there by *each of our congregations'* 12, 70 and 500?

What if the assimilated talmidim used these opportunities to invite people to the weekly or monthly community gatherings on location? What if that led people to come to our Sunday gatherings to conversationally learn how to live a life pleasing to God?

What if our marketing simply used the ongoing theme of "Living Lives Pleasing To God!"? What if we interspersed two or three of the nearly 100 on-location video teachings of Ray Vander Laan that our people might experience the Bible in its historical context? (ThatTheWorldMayKnow.org)

If you're a megachurch, what if the Sunday gatherings began in the auditorium and then broke out into the smaller rooms where five or six of the 500 could lead *conversational discussion* with the groups in each room? 500 ÷ 6 = 83 potential rooms where this could happen each week.

What if our conversational small group time mid-week was led by *more than one* of the 70 or the 500 in the Co-Leadership style described in *Leading*?

As is also described in *Leading*, if we will set the ground rules for respectful conversation (as will be briefly referenced in the next chapter) even the most intense Sunday group discussions with the lost and the immature may be kept safe.

Chapter Four

How To Live A Life Pleasing To God

Go, make talmidim. Don't just baptize them, preach to them, and direct them into small groups of ill-prepared leaders - train them conversationally like Jesus did! Like his apostles did!

How do *you* make disciples? *Talmidim*, not students, not apprentices, not people who take in information and then apply it practically (often errantly) to their life. Not disciples who *call* themselves disciples while *leaning on their own understanding* but are clearly *not* talmidim. *Talmidim.* Like Jesus made talmidim. People who are consumed by their love of the Lord, his text and who know him and his ways intimately.

What is the evidence of your success in developing talmidim? The character and attributes of a talmid are not as difficult to identify as one might think…

What is the biggest obstacle they have to overcome? I can tell you that it is known, but also that it is very rare to find teaching on it. We identify it in great scriptural detail in the *Life* portion of the free book *Life, Love and Leading*. We describe how to overcome it, and include a case study of those who *are accomplishing it* in the *Leading* portion. I can also tell you that we began adopting this obstacle almost immediately after expulsion from Eden. What is it?

Our belief in Hierarchy, Authority and the right to Control people.

As long as we believe in these, we will fail to produce talmidim like Jesus produced talmidim.

The evidence of a true talmid? It is examined scripturally in *Life. Life* is a Bible study that has been used effectively for years with individuals and in small group studies with people from all walks of life. Summarizing that evidence here, you will see adherence to:

- Dominion over the earth, but not over people. (Genesis 1:26-30)
  - Give us a king. (1 Samuel 8:4-22)
  - Jesus said it shall not be so among you. (Mark 10:42-45)
- The Ten Commandments (Exodus 20:3-17)

- Love the Lord your God with all your heart, soul, mind and strength, your neighbor as yourself and one another as I have loved you. (Mark 12:30-31, John 13:34-35)
- "Love" active in service. (John 12:26, Mark 9:35, Mark 10:45, Galatians 5:13, Matthew 20:26-27, 1 Samuel 12:24)
- A heart after the Father in attitudes consistent with the Beatitudes: Jesus' attitudes. (Matthew 5:2-12)
- Fruit of the Spirit language and actions. (Galatians 5:22-24)
- The Unity, character and attributes of John 17.

God's desire is to lead us through each day in one-ness with him, taught by him, to grow us to reflect his character and attributes (John 17) to others more and more, little by little, success by success, glory by glory (2 Corinthians 3:18); conformed to the image of his Son (Romans 8:29); that none should perish (2 Peter 3:9). Jesus did this conversationally and by his servant actions - not by preaching alone. The making of a talmid requires conversational time and service individually, *life-on-life*. As he did with the twelve and as they then did with others.

Over the last 3 decades I have been watching God multiply those he gave myself and others go on to expand his kingdom - life-on-life - with others still.

Life has been used effectively for years with individuals and in small group studies with people from all walks of life: the impoverished, the homeless, present & former prison inmates, struggling believers, wayward believers, in marital & pre-marital counseling, with friends, parents, pastors, mentors and teachers. *Life* helps us think about our conversations together with *hearts* after the Father, the *mind and attitudes* of Christ, *language and actions* that produce *fruit of the Spirit*, and *love* that proves we *care* and are *his*: "A new commandment I give to you, that you love one another: just as I have loved you, you also are to love one another. By this all people will know that you are my talmidim, if you have love for one another."

As with Jesus, we will have groups of people with whom we discuss the kingdom of God, but also with whom we will then spend time individually, conversationally *and in service*. Endeavoring to *become* like Jesus, the evidence of our success or failure will be *talmidim* who more and more:

- Know God's voice and follow. (John 5:19, John 8:28, John 10:27, John 12:49-50, John 14:10)

- Creatively collaborate and participate in accomplishing the will of the Father. (Genesis 2:19-20, 1 Kings 22:19-23, Mark 6:34-44)
- Only say and do what the Father gives them to say and do. (John 5:19, John 8:28, John 12:49-50, John 14:10)
- The elimination of *Anger, Judgement, Condemnation, Hierarchy* and *Manipulate To Control* behaviors from their lives. (Romans 1:28-32, Colossians 3:1-17, Galatians 5:13-26, John 17)
- Are overcoming the temptations and desires of the flesh, their sacrifice nothing compared to Jesus' sacrifice on our behalf. (Romans 1:18-32, Colossians 3:1-17, Galatians 5:13-26, Leviticus 18, Ephesians 5:1-21, James 4:1-12, 1 Peter 2:11-12, Ephesians 2:1-7, 1 John 2:3-6)
- Are *becoming* mature and effective laborers: the 12, the 70 and the 500.

Jesus was willing to start with the 12 and let it expand from there. I know prevailing pastors without a church split in 4 decades who have taken this approach and who now have talmidim making talmidim who are making talmidim. Their approach is summarized in *Life, Love and Leading*.

The Leading portion of Life, Love and Leading discusses beliefs that keep church leaders from taking this approach and, as they continue on as before, therefore scuttle their own efforts to scale - again and again and again.

****

My wife and I have moved many times over the last 45+ years and have therefore attended many churches. As it turns out, God placed us in these that we might observe and have intimate knowledge of the cause of four church splits and, in others, see how his ways avoided them and grew his Kingdom. In each case the splits were caused by hierarchical pastors warring against flesh and blood. In the others, which flourished without splits for four and five decades, iron sharpened iron utilizing the *collective wisdom of all* in Unity and respect.

By rejecting the use of Hierarchy, Control and the use of voting for expediency – they avoided having winners and losers and therefore the sowing of the seeds of us/them and we/they Division.

Conflict seems natural and unavoidable in the *World* Operating System since having winners and losers is just a part of life! Be aware, we use phrases like, “Time is of the essence!” to justify decisive Authoritarian action and/or the call for a vote: “Something must be done! Lead, follow or get out of the way!”.

Synergy finds its foundation in the organizational climate. As long as we utilize polity and organization under the military chain of command, we will be unable to synergistically operate in God’s Unity Operating System and Structure - with us as body parts and Christ the only Head.

As described in *Leading*, there is a way to operate *everything* in The Unity Operating System and Structure. I have seen it work in businesses, churches and non-profits - as have other consultants and authors. God is blessing those of us in these churches, businesses and organizations with synergy and Unity as we operate as follows.

For more background scripture and detail please see both *Life* and *Leading.* Summarizing the above two portions together, true talmidim *and their entities* will evidence:

- Dominion over the earth, but not over people. (Genesis 1:26-30)
    - Give us a king. (1 Samuel 8:4-22)
    - Jesus said it shall not be so among you. (Mark 10:42-45)
- The Ten Commandments (Exodus 20:3-17)
- Love the Lord your God with all your heart, soul, mind and strength, your neighbor as yourself and one another as I have loved you. (Mark 12:30-31, John 13:34-35)
- “Love” active in service. (John 12:26, Mark 9:35, Mark 10:45, Galatians 5:13, Matthew 20:26-27, 1 Samuel 12:24)
- Hearts after the Father in attitudes consistent with the Beatitudes: Jesus’ attitudes. (Matthew 5:2-12)
- Fruit of the Spirit language and actions. (Galatians 5:22-24)
- The Unity, character and attributes of John 17.
- Knowing God’s voice and be following *him.* (John 5:19, John 8:28, John 10:27, John 12:49-50, John 14:10)
- Creative collaboration and participation in accomplishing the will of the Father. (Genesis 2:19-20, 1 Kings 22:19-23, Mark 6:34-44)
- Only saying and doing what the Father gives them to say and do. (John 5:19, John 12:49-50, John 14:10)
- The elimination of *Anger, Judgement, Condemnation, Hierarchy* and *Manipulate To Control* behaviors from their lives. (Romans 1:28-32, Colossians 3:1-17, Galatians 5:13-26, John 17)

- Are overcoming the temptations and desires of the flesh, their sacrifice nothing compared to Jesus' sacrifice on our behalf. (Romans 1:18-32, Colossians 3:1-17, Galatians 5:13-26, Leviticus 18, Ephesians 5:1-21, James 4:1-12, 1 Peter 2:11-12, Ephesians 2:1-7, 1 John 2:3-6)
- That they are *becoming* mature and effective laborers more and more: the 12, the 70 and the 500.

What if a portion of your approach was to put the above up as reference on walls, websites and for use in periodic review during group time? Alongside the statement of operating values below? (These are available for download, poster size, at OneKingdomWorldwide.org. See the *Leading* portion of *Life, Love and Leading* for scriptural support and detail.) Using these and the approach that Pat Lencione clearly describes in The Advantage, even the most intense discussions with the lost may be kept safe:

We are committed to:

- One-ness: Him in us and us in Him
- Acts of Love & Intercession
- Hearts after the Father in attitudes consistent with the Beatitudes: Jesus' attitudes
- Fruit of the Spirit Language & Actions
- Connecting & Inviting
- Relational Mutually Accountable Co-Discipleship
- Development of Balanced Director/Reconciler Teams in Co-Leadership
- Leadership Teams that Do Not Have or Use Hierarchy/Authority
- Unity/Unanimity in Decisions & Actions
- Groups of Teams and Teams of Groups
- Leadership Development at All Levels
- Advisory Forums at ALL levels
  - *Collective* discernment of the Input of ALL People
  - Has God brought us a Leader Out Of Nowhere, now here?
- Facilitating Spirit-Led Self-Selection of Service

What if Sundays became a conversational day around a list of related scriptures? If so, you would be able to facilitate discussion without any significant preparation time. If you did, you could replace the time needed for sermon preparation each week with *conversational life-on-life time* with each of your leaders - with your 12. Perhaps providing them the free *Life, Love and Leading* books as talmidic reference material. What if you made such progress with your 12 that you could add another 12 each year, such that some were *going out* as others were coming in?

What if they then began doing the same with others still, such that at some point you would have 12, 70, and even 500 ready and able to be present at your own "Go" in a community center, park, marketplace, parking lot, homeless camp or even just a street corner? What if they were able to be scattered among the people there like salt, each grain reflecting his light, illuminating their path home…?

What if – minimally in twos - they were to then begin group gatherings with others still? What if each of these new talmidic leaders also initiated individual conversational life-on-life opportunities with the individuals in the group – as you did? First into your congregation, then into the world? Explaining to them what a disciple *really* is and *sending them out*, using their local Community Service And Support Network to find their fit in community service (CSASNetwork.org)? Where they can *serve* while also being yeast, salt and light? (See the *Leading* portion of *Life, Love and Leading* for scriptural support and detail, especially the Epilogue.)

If each one will reach just one each year, we will change our world.

As is described in detail in *Leading*, if we will set the ground rules for respectful conversation using the "Evidence of a Talmid" and "We are committed to:" lists above - (especially the attitudes of the Beatitudes and fruit of the Spirit language and actions) and are further prepared by the Pat Lencione book The Advantage, - even the most intense Sunday group discussions with the lost may be kept safe.

We would do well to reconsider our tradition of an individual teaching to our gatherings by lecture. Rather, as did the synagogues of The Triangle in Jesus' day, let's afford people conversational iron sharpening iron opportunities. Our only requirement should be that they do so with hearts after the Father, humbly postured in the attitudes of the Beatitudes, and that they share thoughts in true fruit of the Spirit language and actions. If we will do so, we just might see our communities begin to flourish once again.

Dear church leaders: If you feel God leading you to continue with preaching on Sundays, at least open it up for an hour of questions, discussion and conversational learning afterwards. Those who don't care that much about what they heard can always leave. Those whose interest was piqued will stay. Remember, the goal is that we *become* mature talmidim - *more and more* like Jesus: learning how to live a life pleasing to God; coming as a child in continual creative conversational worship (prayer) for the accomplishment of the Father's will; hearing his voice and following; sharing how to obey everything he has commanded; seeing, perceiving and being healed.

Chapter Five

We Do Not Battle Against Flesh And Blood

Church leaders are frustrated. For too many, teaching has become a battle or a surrender. Jesus would have neither. His teaching produced thoughtful dialogue. His was not a commentary on the ways of the world, rather his enlightened us on *how to overcome* the world and fulfill the Torah. "How to live a life pleasing to God". He showed us *how*.

I frequently hear church leaders describe an "us versus them" in which they are battling *against* the very flesh and blood *we are to be battling against the principalities and powers for!*

Mark 2:17 I came not to call the righteous, but sinners. Luke 5:32 I have not come to call the righteous, but sinners to repentance."

Some describe themselves as warriors protecting their sheep, but if you first have 12, then 70 and then 500 well trained talmidim, they will have *also* been prepared by the Good Shepherd to identify wolves, *how* to approach them, *how* to inform them and *how* to forewarn them. True talmidim don't need your protection, and if the *immature* sheep are continually being taught conversationally *how* to identify the differing behaviors between sheep and wolves as in the previous chapter, they will be ready and protected *by* this teaching *and* by the power of the Holy Spirit.

Still others who think of themselves as warriors describe their need to convict and rebuke their sheep, shaming them into godly living. But Jesus reserved his convicting and rebuking for the religious leaders of the day, and shaming was never a method used with his sheep. Please remember that one of the reasons Moses was not allowed into Canaan was because of his harsh words to *God's* sheep in Numbers 20:2-13, for *striking* the rock in anger and for the degree of glory he usurped from God as *he took some degree of credit* for giving them water.

Too frequently I hear teaching from the front that rebukes, but why must *the healthy* hear your rebuke? It is, of course, because preaching to the masses is your only chance to convict those beyond your touch. Though *wolves* may be present, why should you expect to reach them? And if the dangerously misinformed approach *you* or you *them* to request individual time, how could you possibly meet with all of them?

Can you instead offer them one of the 12, the 70 or the 500 to meet *individually* to discuss their questions and challenges? The 12, 70 and 500 are the critical portions of what we are to be about! Are you about it? Do you *have* 12 true talmidim in leadership with whom you have a plan for reaching the 70 and the 500? Jesus had a Judas, so too you also may expect some failures.

Counseling groups of people is never effective for the entire group. We will have far greater success in calling the sinners to repentance if we, the 12, the 70 and the 500, will do so individually in life-on-life conversations.

As you continue on after the first 12, some will obviously be more difficult than others, but if they are "here", we are to attempt to train them through ongoing *life-on-life* conversations. Though a portion will eventually reject and run, we (with our 12, our 70 and our 500) are to remain relational and available as they consider their options.

****

I cannot know all things, so God brings me help in the form of people and information. My help is in the name of the Lord, and many are passionate leaders-of-leaders. The Enemy tries to separate us by convincing us to ignore strong-willed leaders. But they know some things we do not know, and we need all of the perspectives we can get. (see *Leading: Working With Alphas*)

Some will be like Peter, Judas, Nicodemus, the Rich Young Ruler, the religious leaders of the day and the pre-Christian Pharisee Saul. We are not to drive them away, like Jesus we are to point them to the Father while answering their questions and concerns! In close proximity to them, speaking to them with the attitudes of the Beatitudes and in fruit of the Spirit language and actions - they will find faith or they will run. That is *their* choice!

Peter was opinionated, not divisive - and passionate - like most of our strong-willed leaders. We just think they are divisive because they are not submitting to (or maybe not acknowledging of) our *hierarchical position* of Authority and the respect that we believe we are entitled to by virtue *of* that position.

This is a syllogism and FAE that may only be supported by the premise of Authority.

We often use syllogism and FAEs to maintain Control over direction:

A syllogism (an inferred conclusion) is a kind of logical argument that applies deductive reasoning to arrive at a conclusion based upon two or more premises that are asserted or assumed to be true.

However, when one premise is the requirement for Hierarchy and Authority, every conclusion that follows will be at least partially false. As we act upon these subtly false deductions, our own subsequent behaviors may be more easily rationalized - the honest result of believing the Enemy's foundational Authority Deception.

Fundamental Attribution Errors occur when we jump to conclusions about a person's *motivation* to behave in an observable way. FAEs block Unity as we attribute ill intentions to another's behavior – thereby helping us to rationalize conflict avoidance strategies. The synergistic potential between complementary personalities is often scuttled by this deception, causing synergistically diverse Body Parts to reject Connectivity.

****

Others will simply be well-intentioned Traditionalists, serving *traditions* in the belief that *these* are *how* they are to support the body of Christ. Not so bad on their own, works may become idols that they serve, doing "good" and therefore *feeling* good about themselves, their identity and their eternity. Something like *faith without works is dead*, they feel they *need* these places of service to feel right about themselves.

In a congregation that is taught *en masse*, there will not be 12, 70 or 500 available for the Traditionalists to receive *individual life-on-life* time from - to understand their error – and will therefore go on entrenching their *works beliefs* into the lives of others they *do* communicate with!

In Meyers-Briggs, these traditionalist personality types are the Guardians that make up 46% of our population. When we better understand how to approach this *half* of our congregants, we will better integrate and synergize their portion of The Body for more productive service - as they support our leaders in service *together* that is transformative.

Until they *become mature talmidim*, the various Traditionalists serving the congregation through altar, music, accoutrements, lawn & landscape, parking, etc. will, over time, become the Traditionalists who block your path to growing the kingdom of God. That they are not talmidim will be evidenced by cliques that are more social than invitational and transformational. Over the decades, absent the life-on-life involvement of you, your 12, your 70 and your 500 - you can expect the Enemy to do anything but use it for good – though the *work* is getting done.

When talmidim are being developed life-on-life, these traditions are allowed to evolve or be eliminated according to the leading of the Holy Spirit, for the benefit of the training and retaining of *talmidim in development*. When these become mature in their understanding, they will be a part of the development of more and more talmidim in the future. Otherwise, as the 12, 70 and the 500 pass on into eternity, who will train the next generation?

A dwindling congregation is symptomatic of a malaise, a short-sightedness, a misunderstanding of appropriate system & structure, and more than anything else – that individuals are not being developed life-on-life to know and understand <u>how</u> to live a life pleasing to God. For if they were, their numbers would be <u>growing</u> as talmidim did what talmidim are to do.

Life, Love and Leading were written to support you with individuals in *life-on-life* time, their *individual* time in worshipful dialogue with Adonai (prayer) and the foundational operating system and structure God has provided us for doing it in Unity as a *fellowship* of believers, a *congregation* of the committed and talmidim who *go* rather than just come.

When it is common to hear our encouragement to request and engage individually in *life-on-life conversations*, many people will come out of hiding. Otherwise, alone and hidden, they will continue to be vulnerable to the Enemy's Deception and be weakened by the wearing downs and tearing downs of life. Absent the Joy of the Lord who is our strength, most will eventually crumble and fall, and fail their friends as well.

As visitors recognize that we are not a place doing business, but one where more and more are *living lives pleasing to God* in the Family of God, the talmidim within our sphere of influence will be more and more successful in drawing in others for training. More than preaching, we will see that the kingdom is growing because of talmidim who are making talmidim in *life-on-life services.*

****

This necessarily includes training up children in the way they should go, that when they grow old they do not depart from it.

Are a portion of your 70 and 500 training children to know his voice? Do you think that this is too scary to do? Do you simply teach them Bible stories and hope that they learn it from their parents?

The Barna group reveals that, on average, children now develop their worldview by age 13 and that 94% of decisions made for Christ happen before the age of 18!

We really need to begin supporting parents in the growing of talmidim who know his voice and follow from childhood!

"Mommy, Daddy, did you see that?" "Yes, Johnny, that was you and God working together! Didn't it feel great to help those people like that?!!! Johnny, you're old enough now for me to help you understand something more about God and how he helps us know what to do and what not to do. Do you remember the other day when you and Bobby both wanted the same toy and you decided to let him play with it first? And last week when..."

"Susie, when you are angry you can always ask God to help you calm down. Did you notice the feeling you had when you were angry? I'm so proud of you that you didn't give in to it!" God helped you to overcome it! Did you notice that you were being helped to decide?

"Tommy, when we are working together with God we will never do anything to harm anyone else." If you ever feel like you are going to, ask God to help you overcome it. He is always right there with you, wherever you go, to help you...

"Sally, what do you want to be when you grow up? You know how we have been talking about how God loves you and is talking to you with his quiet voice to help you? Well, he wants to help you with what you will be when you grow up, too. If you will talk with him about your hopes and dreams, he will

help you with your choices. As you talk with him to understand, he will make your life better than you can possibly imagine.

Jimmy, you're ready for us to start talking with you about how we live our lives in the attitudes of Jesus. These attitudes include humility, having sorrow for others, gentleness with others, a desire for God's righteousness to occur, having mercy on others, making peace with others, and an understanding that many people are going to treat us badly. These attitudes will help us say and do things that will grow relationships of love, joy, peace, patience, kindness, goodness, gentleness, perseverance and self-control. As your parents, we are going to start helping you see when you are living in this way and when you are not. We're also going to start helping you understand how to communicate with people who are using Manipulate To Control behaviors. If you will be willing to do this with us, you will be able to be at Peace even when there is trouble. The more you learn to live in Jesus' ways, the better your life will be!

Chapter Six

Who Do *You* Say That You Are?

As is described and supported in great scriptural detail in *Life* and *Leading*, God's operating system functions in Unity and produces good fruit, fruit of the Spirit. The Enemy's operating system facilitates self-focus, Hierarchy, Authority and Division - producing in-fighting, politics, the development of power, and Corruption.

Separated from God outside of Eden, the Enemy Adam and Eve chose to believe had ongoing access. Engraining the Deception as old as time itself, he has forever since been facilitating a foundational Deception that *we need to take Authority over people*. His hierarchical World Operating System has now become so deeply engrained across the world culturally and throughout history that we do not even realize it is from whence chaos grows.

Scripture identifies that Christ is the Head, our only authority, and he gives us leadership roles that collectively facilitate Wisdom in choosing *together* – producing good fruit and Unity among his people. As explained in *Leading*, even the international consultants for large Fortune 500 multi-national corporations have come around to abandoning authoritarian models based upon the hierarchical military chain of command and are instead teaching the use of God's Unity Operating System – and they have been proving that God's way works best. It's clear, the use of Hierarchy and Authority is out!

In a search for the English word authority in an interlinear Bible, what we find in the original language is that it is only ever used as it applies to that of God or government. The only exception in which God's *people* are described as having authority is in Matthew 10:1.

Matthew 10:1

Jesus called his twelve disciples to him and gave them authority to drive out impure spirits and to heal every disease and sickness.

The word authority has sometimes been added elsewhere by well-meaning Bible translators, but it is not in the original text. In the example below, the ESV includes it but the NIV does not. Though theologians say that the ESV is very reliable (and I agree), this is a case where it is in err. Interlinear Bibles confirm the NIV (and others) to be accurate in this. Try an interlinear search on the internet and see for yourself.

3 John 1:9 ESV

I have written something to the church, but Diotrephes, who likes to put himself first, does not acknowledge our authority.

3 John 1:9 NIV

I wrote to the church, but Diotrephes, who loves to be first, will not welcome us.

His ways are Unity first, inclusive and transparent. The Enemy's way is to divide and conquer to block transparency and gain Control - and that is how he gets what he wants between us – Division. Synergy is a great risk to his schemes, so he tells us that *we* are the one with the *title and position* of Pastor, Teacher, Apostle, Prophet, Evangelist, and that *the office* and the responsibilities *of* that office are *ours* – so we tell others that *they* need to recognize that and back off. But God has warned us that these are not to be our ways. For if they are, they will tempt us toward separation, isolation and individuation.

Though in various settings over the years I have been called Pastor, Teacher, Apostle, Prophet and Evangelist out of respect, I have always asked to be called only by my name. Otherwise, I will be tempted to use that title for my personal benefit.

Matthew 23:8-12

8 But you are not to be called rabbi, for you have one teacher, and you are all brothers. 9 And call no man your father on earth, for you have one Father, who is in heaven. 10 Neither be called instructors, for you have one instructor, the Christ. 11 The greatest among you shall be your servant. 12 Whoever exalts himself will be humbled, and whoever humbles himself will be exalted.

The only instances of a capital letter at the front of the words pastor, teacher, apostle, prophet or evangelist in the Bible refer to Jesus. When did we decide that we should call them *offices* or *positions* and include capital letters as was only done for the Christ? Pastor, Teacher, Apostle, Prophet,

Evangelist, Senior Pastor, CEO Pastor, COO Pastor, Reverend, Dr., MDiv, Teaching Pastor, Deacon, etc. The Bible says that Paul was an apostle and Elijah a prophet, but there are no capital letters calling them Apostle Paul or Prophet Elijah. Shall we elevate ourselves above them?

There is nothing wrong with identifying Body Parts structurally as long as they are simply categories such as teaching pastor, deacon, youth pastor, outreach leader, etc.

Otherwise, the additional danger in the use of *titles and offices* is that the congregants within our sphere of influence, living in a *world* of titles and Authority, will begin to lift us up *over* them. This is a very heady situation in which, having been placed above them *by them*, we just might accept their adulations and slide back into functioning with Leverage and Hierarchically. After all, it is what folks with these trainings expect of us!

****

We are failing together – subtly. We compete, debate, posture, suppress, rationalize, minimize, triangulate. Eyes don't see, ears don't hear. When two leaders meet to discuss a topic of mutual interest what happens? *Positional* circumstances determine if one holds the upper hand, and if so, they will expect to keep it (Authoritarian posture). Whoever thinks they have the greater experience will posture to imply that. Each will <u>*MAN*</u>euver to maintain or improve their position – just as the apostles were doing that day.

Mark 9:33-35

33 And they came to Capernaum. And when he was in the house he asked them, "What were you discussing on the way?" 34 But they kept silent, <u>*for on the way they had argued with one another about who was the greatest*</u>*. 35 And he sat down and called the twelve. And he said to them, "If anyone would be first, he must be* <u>*last of all and servant of all*</u>*."*

Who was greatest among them could only have been important in the determination of who had the most power, and therefore the ability to use it. They were trying to determine the hierarchy of who had Authority over whom.

What if one of them is the Senior Pastor of the church the other attends? What are the tendencies? What is the likelihood for a Unified conclusion?

Similar in giftedness, similar in intellect, similar in capacity, differing in experience and with thousands of years of culture teaching us that there can only be one boss – it is likely that there will be posturing. It is likely to be said, "I am the Pastor.", or, "As Pastor I…" It is what is done. But God's way is better.

When we are mature, balanced and United with him in our hearts, souls and minds, we may more effectively communicate and discern the *collective wisdom* God offers us *together*. Practice utilizing *fruit of the Spirit* language and actions that you more and more *become* a talmid of Jesus, and therefore a more effective communicator doing the will of the Father. Kindly, Gently, Perseveringly, Peaceably and with Goodness. As we learn to live with hearts after the Father and in the attitudes of the Beatitudes (Jesus' attitudes), this posture and humility will prepare us for fruit of the Spirit language and actions in each and every interaction.

As is described in *Life* and *Leading*, we must learn his ways of Relational Mutual Accountability in Co-Discipleship if we will *sustainably* Connect our brothers and sisters to The Body. As is further described in *Life*, it might accurately be said that the depth of our trust and understanding will bring us to the depth of our faith in one another. And that the depth of our love will be based upon these. Develop trust in Relational Mutual Accountability and Co-Discipleship - and then watch God work.

His ways are Unity first, inclusive and transparent. The Enemy's way is to take Control, perhaps by Divide and Conquer, for the blocking of transparency - and that is how he gets what he wants between us – Division.

Synergy is a great risk to his schemes.

Chapter Seven

Servant Talmidim

Clearly, as is identified with exhaustive supporting scriptural detail in *Life*, Jesus only said and did what the Father gave him to say and do. As talmidim we are to do the same. His heart was after the Father and his desire was to do all of his will.

"Do this in remembrance of me."

Most of my life my remembrance during Communion has been of his suffering and death on my behalf. The whipping, the beatings, the crown of thorns, the nails, the mocking, the anguish, hanging there, rejected, in excruciating pain…

…and finally, death. His saving sacrifice.

But, I think, this is not what he wants most to be remembered for. Time after time throughout his life he pointed people to our Father in heaven. It doesn't make sense to me that what he wants to do now is point us to himself rather than our Father. No, it seems more likely that what he wants us to remember about him is that he was one *who only said and did what our Father gave him to say and do.*

Throughout his entire life. All the way to the end of it:

He trained the 12, setting into motion the 70, the 500 and the making of talmidim in every nation on earth.

He went to Jerusalem, knowing what would happen there.

He told Judas to get on with it.

He went to Gethsemane and waited for his Accusers in prayerful obedience.

He asked the Father if there might be another way.

He went willingly when they came for him.

He endured and accomplished the purpose for which he was born.

He did *all* his Father's will.

Having taken responsibility for both God and Man as the God-Man, he provided us all a pathway to reconciliation *with* the Father and *into* the Family of God.

We have been told to do the same for others. Paraphrasing his instructions to us he said: "Go, show them *how to live a life pleasing to God*, baptizing them into the life-changing internal Presence of the Father and of the Son and of the Holy Spirit, teaching them to observe all that I have commanded you. It will be for them the pathway to reconciliation with the Father, into the Family of God and therefore *into their abundant joy filled life with us together - eternally*."

Go help people become like me in all the nations...

But how can we help people *become like him* if we aren't really *like him* ourselves? Lean not on your own understanding (Proverbs 3:1-8), but by every word from the mouth of God (Matthew 4:3-4, Deuteronomy 8:1-3).

Unfortunately, so many of us have been focusing upon baptizing and lecturing and have been neglecting the making of talmidim. We have watered down the foundational aspects of who God is and what he desires of us such that our children hardly know him, our families are *becoming* weaker, and the division and degradation of our nation is on the increase.

What if we were to change our approach so as to better facilitate hearts after the Father, emphasizing our need to use words and actions growing fruit of the Spirit? In Jesus' attitudes of the Beatitudes? In the image of God? In the ways of God?

We tend to give people the facts and the logic and fight to persuade them for saving faith and helpful actions. As we keep their brains engaged in thinking it all through, a portion walk away, feeling something amiss.

It is not all that difficult to learn to live with hearts after the Father walking in the attitudes of Jesus (the Beatitudes). As we do, this posture and humility prepares us for fruit of the Spirit language and actions always and everywhere.

Our nation is deeply divided, with many angry "Christians" part of the problem. Romans 1, Colossians 3 and Galatians 5 are but a few of the references that tell us that what we *are* doing is what we *are not* to be doing - *and that those who (continue to) do such things will not inherit the kingdom of God* (Galatians 5:21).

We must now, more and more, offer ourselves up as a work in process to the Father, Son and Holy Spirit - *with unveiled face, beholding the glory of the Lord, and be transformed into the same image from one degree of glory to another*. That we make talmidim, doing the will of the Father.

Stating our agreement with him regarding his kingdom and will, we are somehow participating with him to cause that which has not yet been caused, release that which has not yet been released and/or fulfill that which is in the process of being fulfilled. We are collaborators co-operating, him in us spiritually and us in him spiritually, with us in the physical creatively participating with him to bring the spiritual into earthly manifestation.
Establishing his kingdom on earth as it is in heaven - in people –
his will being done: that all might come to know him, love him and join him,
and thereby enter into the Family of God.
That none should perish.

"Do this in remembrance of me."
He only said and did as Our Father told him.
He endured, and accomplished the purpose for which he was born.
He did his Father's will.
May it be true of us!

On our minds and in our hearts before our meals each day, may we remember Jesus pointing to our Father, speaking of his will and of the Holy Spirit who will flow through us to accomplish it. As we give thanks, may we continue to agree with the Father *as often as we drink it* (1 Corinthians 11:25) that *his will* be done in our life. Because eternity in view, our sacrifice will be over in the blink of an eye – and ours nothing compared to his.

Over two thousand years ago Jesus started conversationally with just twelve. Through him, in him and with him, hundreds of millions, maybe several billion, now know him today. Surely there is someone with whom we might offer to start meeting conversationally each week. Some of us with at least a few. Others with more than a few.

Let us endeavor to offer the talmidic approach,
that we might grow hearts after our Father.

****

Jesus made it clear to us that the Father's will is that we go make talmidim of all nations, not just teach them Beth Sephir and Beth Midrash (in our case, the whole Bible). Therefore, like Jesus, our *service* will open the door to sharing our *testimony* about the love of God for all humanity.

We will not be successful in making talmidim if we are not teaching and training *individual* talmid to hear God's voice and be one with him, him in us and us in him - and follow in the *Father's* will for their lives. Serving where *he* sends them, their testimony will be sufficient for whoever he puts in their path. *Each one reaching one*, the world will be changed. *Each one reaching one each year*, we will more quickly accomplish the Great Commission.

It is not our job to send them anywhere, our job is to make talmidim who will follow the leading of the Holy Spirit to where they are being sent. While church projects that organize to serve the community are a part of what we are to be doing, the growing of individual talmid who are going where God sends them is primary.

As talmidim grow in their understanding, they will *become* sheep who know God's voice and follow. As they *serve* in relationship with others, with hearts after the Father and the mind and attitudes of Christ, we and they may expect that the Spirit will lead them into what the Father would have them say and/or do in any situation.

As salt is scattered in this way across our communities, every grain reflecting the light of God's love, *more and more people will be led into lifesaving relationship*. However, the critical first step is that our churches *become* talmidic training centers that *send.* Not just places where people *go* each week, or as surveys indicate, only occasionally during the year.

Do you believe that God has created works for all of us in advance (Ephesians 2:10)? Then as you also acknowledge Ephesians 4, telling us that the role of the leader is to equip/prepare/facilitate the people to acts of service, why not be facilitating administrative system & structure that makes it happen!

Chapter Eight

The Community Service and Support Network

Our nation is deeply divided, with many angry "Christians" part of the problem, Pastors included. Romans 1, Colossians 3 and Galatians 5 are but a few of the references that tell us that what we *are* doing is what we are *not* to be doing - and that *those who (continue to) do such things will not inherit the kingdom of God.* (Galatians 5:21)

For those who might just be willing, are we available to lead them into a greater depth of understanding of *his* ways, a more *intimate* walk *with* him, for fruit of the Spirit conversations in the attitudes of the Beatitudes, and in the growth and change described in 2 Corinthians 3:14-18? They will otherwise continue on as blind as the religious of *that* day.

If we want to win souls, our only chance is by making God's ways our ways and his will our will. Let us endeavor to offer *the talmidic approach, becoming more and more like Jesus*, growing hearts after our Father.

****

As we close a net of eight churches each day in the USA, we would do well to remember that we have departed from the efficiencies of the "Go" and are rather suffering the expenses of telling people to "Come". In our region of 300,000 people, we have over half a billion dollars of churches and property to maintain. Each year, the operating budgets for those properties cost over 140 million dollars.

The Roman emperor Julian, one of the fiercest second-century persecutors of early Christians (whom the early church aptly referred to as Julian the Apostate) admitted in disgust to a friend that he couldn't stop the Church from growing no matter how many he jailed or killed because 'these infernal Galileans feed our poor in addition to their own.' Historian Eberhard Arnold notes, 'Most astounding to the outside observer was the extent to which poverty was overcome in the vicinity of the communities. Christians spent more money in the streets than the followers of other religions spent in their temples.'." J. D. Greear, Gaining by Losing: Why the Future Belongs to Churches that Send (Zondervan, 2005), 126.

In our region, 20% of our 300,000 people have an income which is below the poverty level: 60,000 people. What if we rather supported and developed non-profits with some of the 140 million dollars we now spend annually to operate and maintain our churches? What if our churches came together and crossed denominational lines in John 17 Unity? What if we had half as many buildings and 70 million dollars more for non-profits?

As a net of eight churches close each day in the USA, their annual budgets disappear, too. What if we began to hold conversations together about the efficient use of the resources God has provided? Before they are gone…

More importantly, when talmidim "Go" to our non-profits to serve, support and do what talmidim are to be doing, lives are forever changed, healed and can become productive talmidim themselves. If we will train up talmidim instead of disciples, students and apprentices, we will transform our communities as talmidim do what talmidim are to be doing!

During the last 40 years I have been working to unite God's people to more productive service in their communities. This has included my collaboration with three different national initiatives that hoped to utilize the internet in doing so. They spent millions of dollars in development of the *what* while missing the point of the *who*. Much has been learned over the last 40 years, and I am sorry to say that the leaders of these initiatives have been mostly unsuccessful.

Learning from that experience, we have paid for the development of a free web platform designed for the *who*. What we know is that people may serve a needy cause for a while, but they will remain with causes that touch their heart as they serve rewardingly alongside people with similar passion - synergizing their diverse skillsets. If we will ever align and engage the people in our communities to service that truly transforms, it will be because we have facilitated our people in finding those with whom their passion and interests align. Simply said, we need to flow people and their diverse skillsets to the non-profits that best match their passion and interests.

The site we have developed is a *free* volunteer Human Resources Department for communities as a whole. It helps people to quickly sort through the myriad of community service options so as to be able to select a *personalized passion-aligned service involvement* with any church or non-profit. It utilizes Service Opportunity Descriptions that clarify the work and time involved.

These are supported by individuals we call Connectors who volunteer their time to vet and Connect people on behalf and in support of a given non-profit. Connectors are passion-aligned individuals who work to help Executive Directors be able to *redirect funds from ancillary expenses* and *add mission critical volunteer roles* toward increasing the output of mission.

If we will transform our communities, we need to have an *aligned* organizational vision *for our communities* that is broader than our *individual organizational* efforts. We have been failing at this for decades via a variety of well-meaning platforms and programs. Now, sometime in 2026, the Community Service and Support Network will be online at CSASNetwork.org with this very simple yet profound approach. The *free* CSASNetwork site will help people community-wide quickly sort through *personalized* community service options so as to be able to easily self-select a *passion-aligned service involvement* with any church or non-profit.

The Community Service and Support Network site will include all that is needed for faithful founders in any city to quickly birth *their own local site* on the CSASNetwork site. Organized into the 4 Groups and 12 Teams as is described in *Leading*, any city of any size will be able to birth and maintain access *for free*. Everything needed to support local founders in the development of the initial 4 Groups and for expansion into the 12 Teams is being included. The last chapter of *Leading*, the Epilogue, helps us imagine the great value that utilizing the Community Service and Support Network site offers.

Considering all of our unique callings, we will better Connect people when we provide a Whole Body System & Structure that additionally aids in *Self-Selection* via a CSASNetwork site. Facilitating Connection by every supporting ligament according to their personal discernment of *God's* leading, people will less frequently *Self-Select out* and more often get *in* and Self-Select to *stay* in. Accomplish your will, O God!

Scattered like salt across our communities and found, as Jesus was, *in service to one another*, each individual grain reflecting the light of God's love, *more and more people will be led into lifesaving relationship* – and our congregations and communities will be restored.

However, the critical first step is that our churches become talmidic training centers that send. Not just places where people go each week, or as surveys indicate, only occasionally during the year.

****

Could it be that preaching is the repellant to our generation, the reason we are closing a net of 8 churches each day in the USA?

At least in school, students may raise their hands to ask a question. When the doubter cannot raise their hand to ask a question frustration builds. Over time these fresh fish stop coming.

Preaching belongs in public, the way Jesus did it. There, the curious fresh fish – the uncured – may hang around to talk with the cured. The piquing of curiosity there draws people in to fellowships for the opportunity to have more questions answered by the cured – not just by the pastor – by the entire fellowship. The "schooled" fish.

Most fresh fish are not interested in hearing from some book that we say will help them, they want a personal interaction for a period of time to answer their questions and assuage their concerns. Everyone in the fellowship MUST have a level of interest in seeking out and opening up to the fresh fish that swim in for a look – and be offering them that period of time.

Fish who have been caught will become interested in the deeper curing available in bible studies.

Many un-caught curious fish who occasionally swim through Sunday services nationally are not interested in being preached at so they don't come back. That is why what we call "attractional church" is "working". It is entertainment. People come back for the show and are able to walk out afterwards with a good feeling. Surveys show that most find other attractional churches to go to when the ones they are in go stale – though the "core" remain.

Wandering fish go from congregation to congregation (attractional or not) from time to time until they stop coming altogether. Eventually, surveys say, the reason they stop is that their insights say that churches are just another business spending their money on their "club". They say, "I hear that Jesus said "Go", but where are they going? Where is all the money going?"

Public data for our region shows we have half a billion dollars worth of church properties spending 140 million dollars annually to maintain their "operations".

The uncured fish are not finding any compelling reason to "go" to church.

Jesus is "truly attractional" in personal ways. His is not entertainment. His is not "preaching to the choir". He "sends" his people out into the world, into the local ocean, to catch fish and bring them home for healing. That is what true *talmidim* want to do, with others who want to do the same. We rarely go out fishing, our traditions are driving away the fresh fish who do come, and our families and nation are in disintegration mode because of it.

Matthew 13:14-15
14 Indeed, in their case the prophecy of Isaiah is fulfilled that says:
"'"You will indeed hear but never understand,
and you will indeed see but never perceive."
15 For this people's heart has grown dull,
and with their ears they can barely hear,
and their eyes they have closed,
lest they should see with their eyes
and hear with their ears
and understand with their heart
and turn, and I would heal them.'

Our people have been going to church for 5, 10, 20, 30, 40 years and more and most still do not go fishing. Jesus had a three year "catch and release" program for the 12. If we have been making talmidim, most *would have become* mature talmidim by now, be out fishing, and would be making talmidim who are making talmidim who are making talmidim… and we would not be closing a net of eight churches each day here in the USA. Our people should *be* mature talmidim by now…

Restating from Chapter Two:

His three-year focus on training the 12 set into motion their activity with the 70, them with the 500 and the making of talmidim in every nation on earth.

Hebrews 5:11-6:3
11 About this we have much to say, and it is hard to explain, since you have become dull of hearing. 12 For though by this time you ought to be teachers, you need someone to teach you again the basic principles of the oracles of God. You need milk, not solid food, 13 for everyone who lives on milk is

unskilled in the word of righteousness, since he is a child. 14 But solid food is for the mature, for those who have their powers of discernment trained by constant practice to distinguish good from evil. 6:1-3 Therefore let us leave the elementary doctrine of Christ <u>*and go on to maturity*</u>*, not laying again a foundation of repentance from dead works and of faith toward God, 2 and of instruction about washings, the laying on of hands, the resurrection of the dead, and eternal judgment. 3 And this we will do if God permits.*

****

When Jesus said go and make talmidim of all nations, he did not say go and teach people Beth Sephir and Beth Midrash (the Tanakh) so that they could practically apply the information to their lives, he said to go help people *become* like him! Between the *what to know* and the *how to live*, he spent more time on the *how – how to live a life pleasing to God.*

He can make us fishers of men, women and children again – if we will collectively follow him on the *talmidic* adventure. As we give up our failing traditions of Sunday preaching and hierarchical organization, the God I know and have seen at work doing so for decades, will bring about healing through *relational conversational learning*.

When we send service minded talmidim (instead of disciples, students and apprentices) into our communities as yeast, salt and light, we will transform our communities as talmidim do what talmidim are to be doing!

What if we had an easy way for mature talmidim to find a passion-aligned non-profit to serve and go fishing in? Conversation is easy for passion-aligned people. What if we matured talmidim such that they had the confidence and courage to use the tools in the *Life* book to relationally develop an interest in the fish around them?

Chapter Nine

Aligning Your Community In Service That Transforms

In *Leading*, we imagine the possibilities when tapping into the potential of 20% more people in a given church, and 10% more in a community of 300,000. If you could tap the non-paid potential of these, the Full-Time Equivalents (FTEs) would be worth tens of millions of dollars in equivalent payroll.

The average payroll of an entire city government for a community of 300,000 people may include 1500 people at an approximate cost of $75,000,000. If you could bring an additional 1500 Full-Time Equivalents (FTEs) through engaging more people in Supportive Service what would that be worth? $75,000,000, yes, but it would be worth much more in terms of the lives of the people those additional FTEs would touch. And what would that be worth in your community? Imagine the value of a reduction in crime, violence, poverty, teen pregnancies, illiteracy, unemployment and welfare. This is what the CSASNetwork.org site is all about helping you do.

- 1500 paid staff averaging $50K per year (including benefits) equals $75,000,000 per year and (working 40 hours per week 50 weeks per year) 3,000,000 hours per year.
- 30,000 more people (10% of the population) in service giving 100 hours per year (2 hours/week) equals 3,000,000 hours per year – a value of $75,000,000.

If you developed a culture in your community whereby more people gave an average of just 50 hours per year of effectively engaged service time – what would that be worth *in* your community? *To* your community? *For* your community?

If we are truly leaders of leaders, if he has set us over much, we are the ones responsible to facilitate more engagement from the inactive. If we will do this, it will necessarily require more unpaid high-capacity large-scale leaders (as described in *Leading*) than we are welcoming now. It will also require an all-encompassing Structure upon which we will make Connections to the whole Body of Christ, Christ as the Head – and life-on-life service and conversations.

Isaiah 43:19
Behold, I am doing a new thing; now it springs forth,
do you not perceive it?

For decades now, in cities all across our nation, there have been countless good-faith efforts to involve more people in community-wide collaborative service. The unique Community Service And Support Network approach includes a wealth of information to assist you in supporting these city-wide collaborations. The time is now. The fields are ripe with harvest. But if we will be successful at the community scale, we had better be practicing it ourselves and introducing it in our churches first. Growing talmidim: the 12, the 70 and the 500.

As we develop talmidim who develop talmidim who develop talmidim, *we* will be the ones who reverse the trend mentioned in the first chapter. As churches *become* talmidic training centers that *send* - more and more talmidim will be scattered like salt across our communities in passion aligned service. As each grain reflects the light of God's love, *more and more people will be led into lifesaving relationship* – and our communities will be restored.

As we end this short summary of *Life, Love and Leading*, we also summarize for you below what we identified both there and here. These bullet points help to move us more and more toward *actualizing* talmidim in Adonai-ical Unity that connects ALL body parts by every supporting ligament. Iron sharpening iron, balanced wholistically through the power of the Spirit and informed collectively by the Wisdom of God, we are better able to collectively discern the Father's will for us. We believe these to be God honoring and necessary as we follow him to make his will happen:

(The following references and charts have been formatted for printing as posters and are available for viewing and download online at: OneKingdomWorldwide.org)

True talmidim will evidence:

- Dominion over the earth, but not over people. (Genesis 1:26-30)
  - Give us a king. (1 Samuel 8:4-22)
  - Jesus said it shall not be so among you. (Mark 10:42-45)
- The Ten Commandments (Exodus 20:3-17)
- Love the Lord your God with all your heart, soul, mind and strength, your neighbor as yourself and one another as I have loved you. (Mark 12:30-31, John 13:34-35)

- "Love" active in service. (John 12:26, Mark 9:35, Mark 10:45, Galatians 5:13, Matthew 20:26-27, 1 Samuel 12:24)
- Hearts after the Father in attitudes consistent with the Beatitudes: Jesus' attitudes. (Matthew 5:2-12)
- Fruit of the Spirit language and actions. (Galatians 5:22-24)
- The Unity, character and attributes of John 17.
- Knowing God's voice and be following *Him*. (John 5:19, John 8:28, John 10:27, John 12:49-50, John 14:10)
- Creative collaboration and participation in accomplishing the will of the Father. (Genesis 2:19-20, 1 Kings 22:19-23, Mark 6:34-44)
- Only saying and doing what the Father gives them to say and do. (John 5:19, John 12:49-50, John 14:10)
- The elimination of *Anger, Judgement, Condemnation, Hierarchy* and *Manipulate To Control* behaviors from their lives. (Romans 1:28-32, Colossians 3:1-17, Galatians 5:13-26, John 17)
- Are overcoming the temptations and desires of the flesh, their sacrifice nothing compared to Jesus' sacrifice on our behalf. (Romans 1:18-32, Colossians 3:1-17, Galatians 5:13-26, Leviticus 18, Ephesians 5:1-21, James 4:1-12, 1 Peter 2:11-12, Ephesians 2:1-7, 1 John 2:3-6)
- That they are *becoming* mature and effective laborers more and more: the 12, the 70 and the 500.

We are committed to Unity:

- One-ness: Him in us and us in Him
- His Unity Operating System and Structure for The Body
- Personal Wholeness
- Hearts after the Father in attitudes consistent with the Beatitudes: Jesus' attitudes!
- Fruit of the Spirit Language & Actions
- Acts of Love & Intercession
- Connecting & Inviting
- Relational Mutually Accountable Co-Discipleship
- Development of Balanced Director/Reconciler Teams in Co-Leadership
- Leadership Teams that Do Not Have or Use Hierarchy/Authority
- Unity/Unanimity in Decisions & Actions
- Groups of Teams and Teams of Groups
- Leadership Development at All Levels
- Advisory Forums at ALL levels
  - Collective Discernment of the Input of ALL People
  - Has God brought us a Leader Out Of Nowhere, now here?
- Facilitating Spirit-Led Self-Selection of Service

We are committed to identifying:

- The Leaders-of-Leaders Being Raised Up for the Initiatives of the Day
- Internally Focused Christ Followers Strengthening the Fellowship
- Externally Focused Christ Followers Engaged in the Community

We are committed to:

Facilitating Spirit-Led Self-Selection of Service

Operations Passion:

- *Administration*: Integration of Teams, Leader Support, Office & Information Systems!
- *Generosity, Fund Development & Financial Oversight*: Stewardship & Financial Support!
- *Leadership Development*: Leader Growth & Support!

Human Services Passion:

- *Education*: Teaching, Training, Learning & Growing!
- *Family Life & Relationships*: Help build strong families & relationships!
- *Life Change, Recovery & Restoration*: Families in Crisis & Recovery for Individuals!

Systems Support & Integration Passion:

- *Celebrations*: Praise & Worship God, Thank People for their Service!
- *Creative Communications*: Explain, Market & Promote!
- *Connections*: Welcome, Connect People to People & Groups of People, Volunteers, Paid Staff!
- *Science & Technology*: Integration of Technological Systems, Engineering, Life Science, etc!

Physical Assets Passion:

- *Environment & Beautification*: Let's keep our surroundings comfortable & beautiful!
- *Property Oversight, Maintenance & Development*: Maintain, Build, Improve, Expand!

Developing Personal Wholeness as God Grows Me

My Operations

- *Administration:* Creation of Income and Compliance with Laws, Banking & Information Systems
- *Generosity & Financial:* Giving where God Leads me to Give; Strengthening my Financial Situation
- *Leadership Development:* Grow my Leadership Ability & Support those I Lead

My Human Service

- *Education:* Learning & Growing; Teaching & Training
- *Family Life & Relationships:* Strengthening and Growing in my Love and Care for Others
- *Life Change, Recovery & Restoration:* Overcoming my Personal Issues; Strengthening People in Crisis & Recovery

My Relationships Support & Integration

- *Celebrate:* Praise & Worship God for What He Is Doing, Thank People for their Service
- *Creatively Communicate:* Explain, Share & Promote the Advancement of the Kingdom of God
- *Connect:* Welcome People; Connect with People; Connect People with Other People; Connect Groups of People
- *Science & Technology:* Utilize Technology, Understand Life Science, be Attentive to my Health

My Physical Assets

- *Environment & Beautification:* Let's Keep our Surroundings Comfortable & Beautiful
- *Property Oversight, Maintenance & Development:* Take Good Care of What I Have, Build, Repair, Improve, Expand

Developing Personal Wholeness & Holiness as God Grows Me

On our path to godliness

Unity Builders: In Humility & Love *The Spirit of the Lord offers freedom, so we:*		**Unity Busters: In Fear of Loss** *In our attempt to Control, we:*
◊ Inform with Gentleness	←	◊ Accuse, Judge, Condemn to Justify our Demands
◊ Encourage with Kindness	←	◊ Use Blame, Anger and Malice to Threaten and Coerce
◊ Explain with grace in Peace	←	◊ Use Shame & Silence to subtly Threaten Abandonment
◊ Share with compassion in Goodness	←	◊ Use our Voice to Threaten Vengeance, Retaliation, Retribution
◊ Describe with hope the Joyful outcome available	←	◊ Rationalize that our divisive actions were caused by them
◊ Train to produce Patience & Perseverance	←	◊ In Pride & frustration, Lie & Deceive (…for their own good)
◊ Coach to develop Self Control	←	◊ Abuse whatever Power we may think we have

I do not have or use authority over people. I do not tell people what to do. I am committed to:

- Being Taught and Trained By Jesus
- Being Led by the Holy Spirit
- Allowing the Father in me to do his Works, that I not enter into temptation and be delivered from evil.
- Attitudes consistent with the Beatitudes
- Fruit of the Spirit language & actions: Love, Joy, Peace, Patience, Kindness, Goodness, Gentleness, Perseverance, Self-Control
- Hearing out all advice and input so as to discern if it is God helping me
- Seeking out the collective wisdom God will provide me personally and us together, that we discern *his* direction.
- Relational Mutually Accountable Co-Discipleship: Supporting each other in *becoming*, as talmidim of Jesus Christ
- Director/Reconciler Co-Leadership in groups of teams and teams of groups
- Inviting & Connecting the inactive
- Facilitating Self-Selection for service

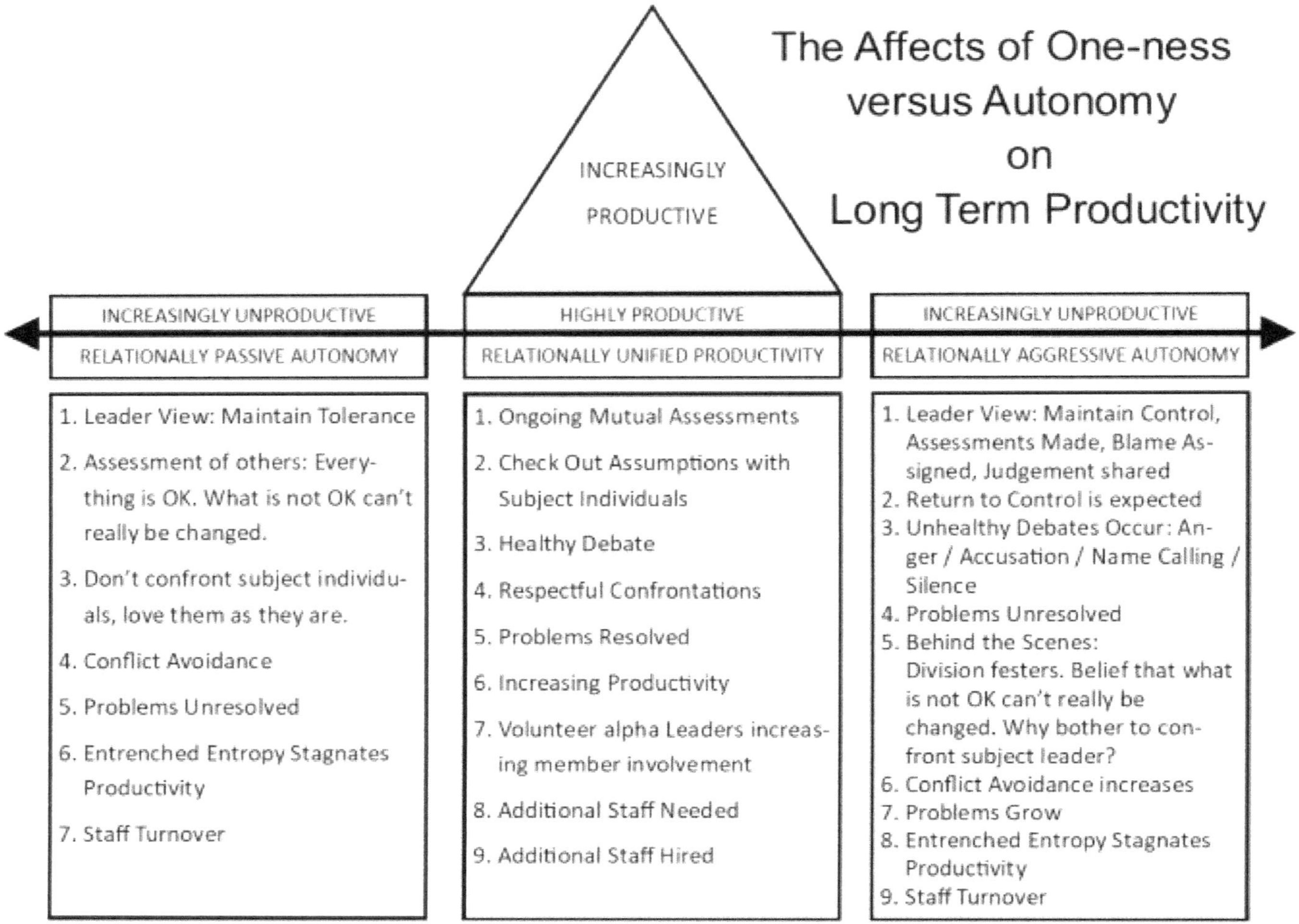

The Affects of One-ness versus Autonomy on Long Term Productivity

INCREASINGLY PRODUCTIVE

INCREASINGLY UNPRODUCTIVE RELATIONALLY PASSIVE AUTONOMY	HIGHLY PRODUCTIVE RELATIONALLY UNIFIED PRODUCTIVITY	INCREASINGLY UNPRODUCTIVE RELATIONALLY AGGRESSIVE AUTONOMY
1. Leader View: Maintain Tolerance 2. Assessment of others: Everything is OK. What is not OK can't really be changed. 3. Don't confront subject individuals, love them as they are. 4. Conflict Avoidance 5. Problems Unresolved 6. Entrenched Entropy Stagnates Productivity 7. Staff Turnover	1. Ongoing Mutual Assessments 2. Check Out Assumptions with Subject Individuals 3. Healthy Debate 4. Respectful Confrontations 5. Problems Resolved 6. Increasing Productivity 7. Volunteer alpha Leaders increasing member involvement 8. Additional Staff Needed 9. Additional Staff Hired	1. Leader View: Maintain Control, Assessments Made, Blame Assigned, Judgement shared 2. Return to Control is expected 3. Unhealthy Debates Occur: Anger / Accusation / Name Calling / Silence 4. Problems Unresolved 5. Behind the Scenes: Division festers. Belief that what is not OK can't really be changed. Why bother to confront subject leader? 6. Conflict Avoidance increases 7. Problems Grow 8. Entrenched Entropy Stagnates Productivity 9. Staff Turnover

The above references, as well as the charts on the following pages, have been formatted for printing as posters and are available for viewing and download online at:

www.OneKingdomWorldwide.org

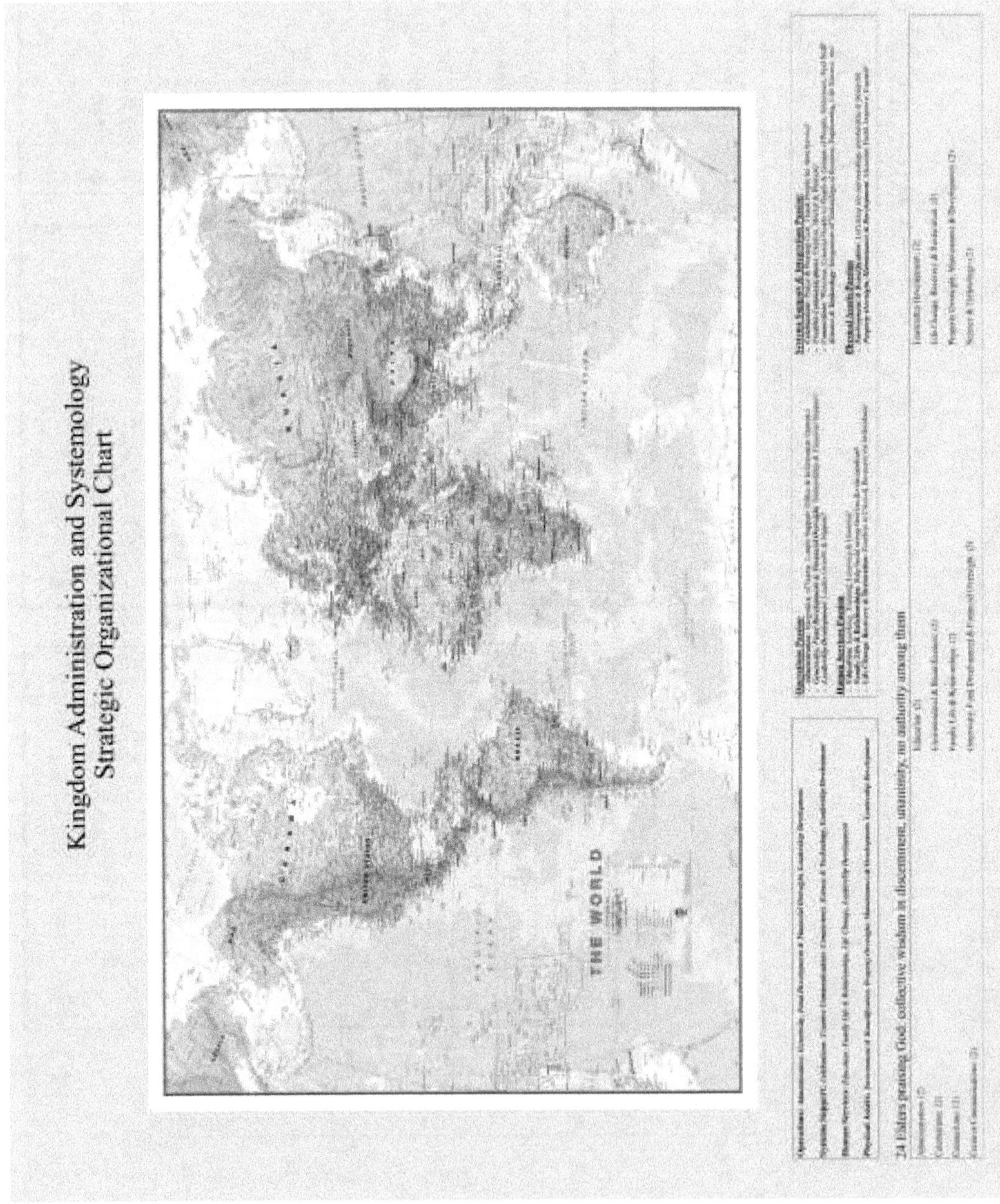

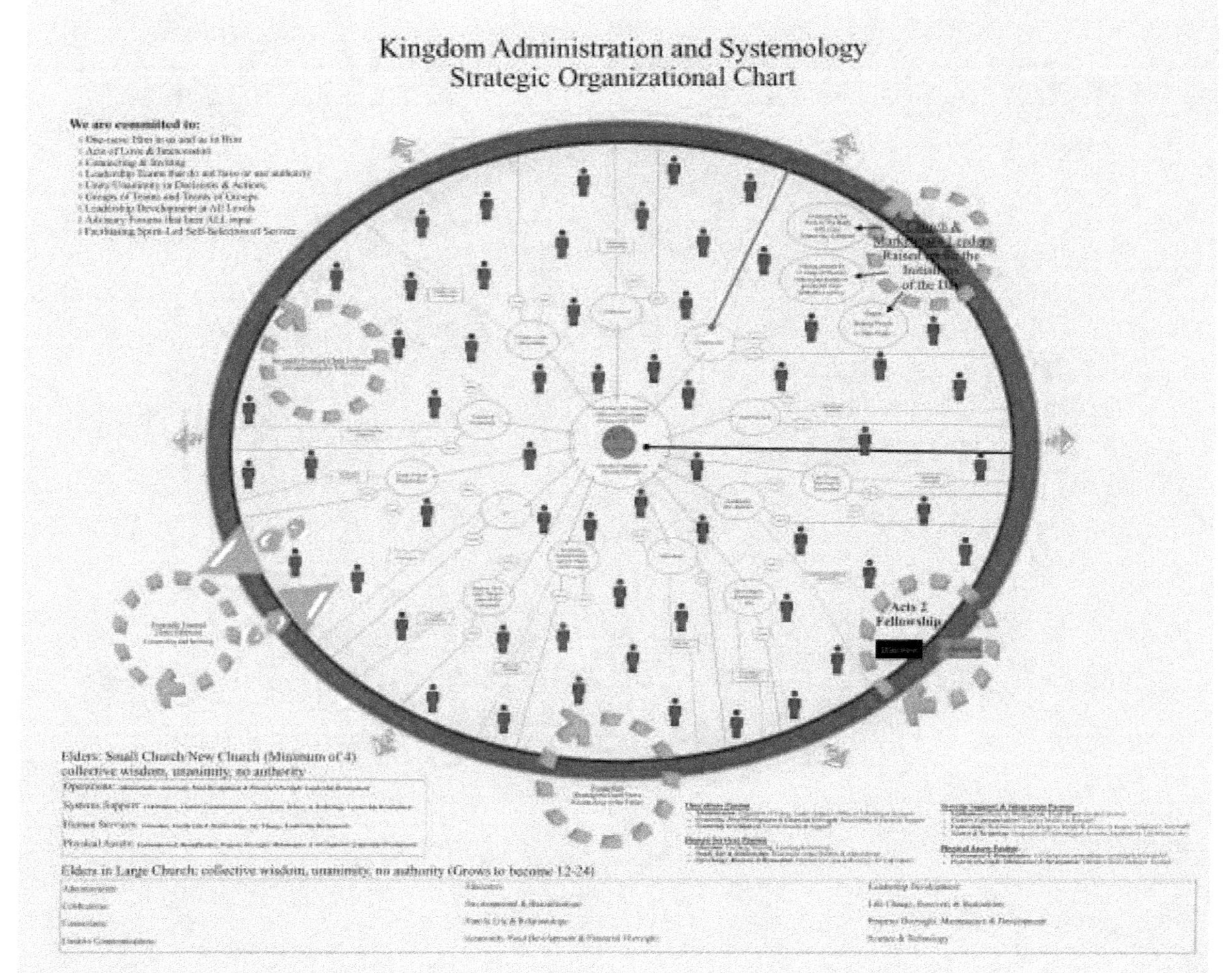

Kingdom Administration and Systemology
Strategic Organizational Chart
We are committed to:
Acts 2
Fellowship
Elders: Small Church/New Church (Minimum of 4)
collective wisdom, unanimity, no authority
Elders in Large Church: collective wisdom, unanimity, no authority (Grows to become 12-24)

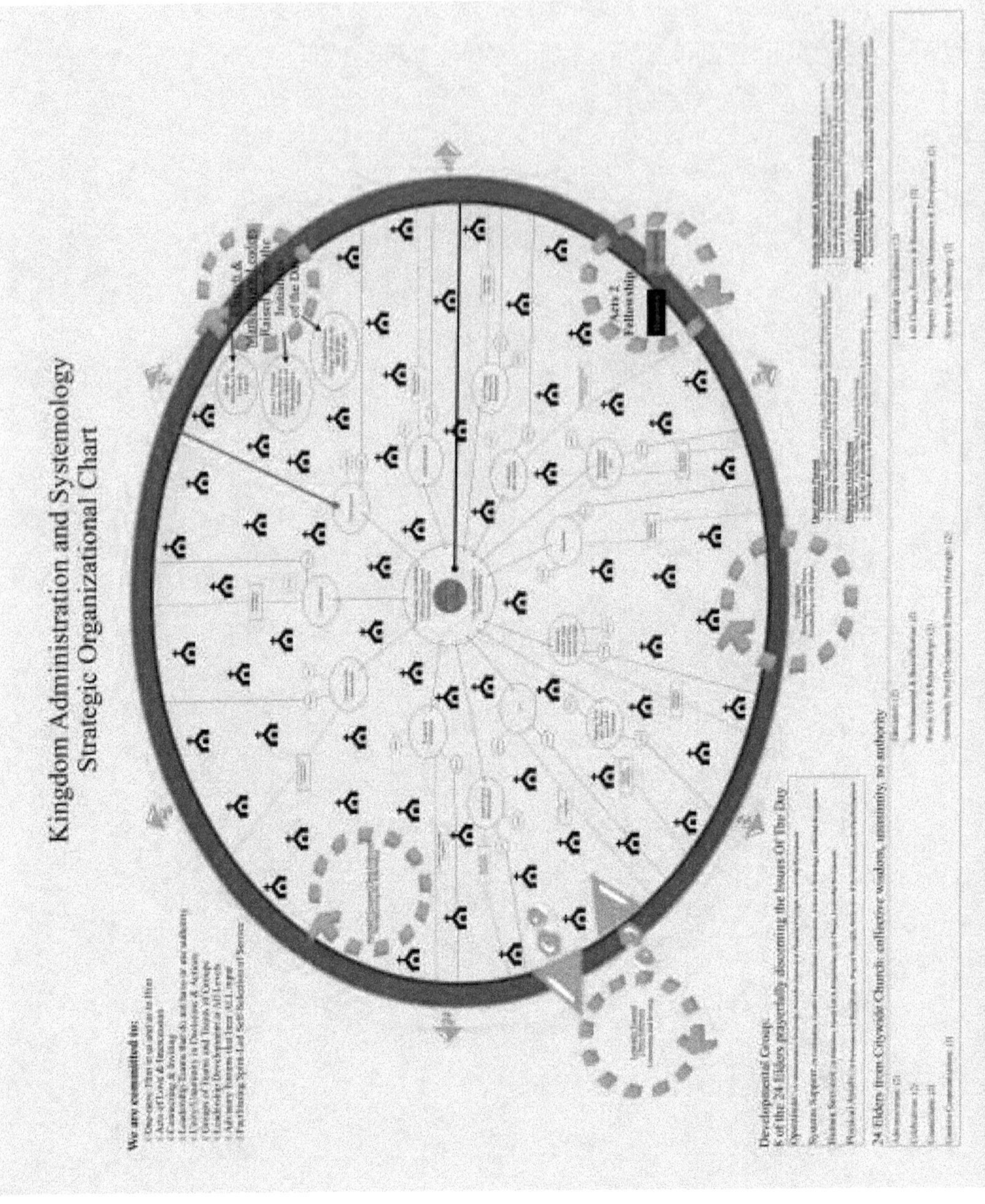

To receive additional free copies please contact:
Ricky Kroeger
One Kingdom Worldwide
One@OneKingdomWorldwide.org

PDF files of this book may be legally shared. Revised March 2026

www.ingramcontent.com/pod-product-compliance
Lightning Source LLC
LaVergne TN
LVHW010945110826
845149LV00013B/2754

* 9 7 9 8 9 9 4 5 8 3 9 0 6 *